MELVIN

WRESTLING WITH THE *Ring* INSIDE OF ME!

PURPOSEFUL TOOLS TO ENCOURAGE THE MAN AND BODY OF CHRIST

KINGDOM BOOKS

Columbia, South Carolina, USA

Published by *KB&G*
From Kingdom Book & Gift LLP
Columbia, South Carolina, USA
www.wix.com/trends/kingdombookandgift

Printed in the U.S.A.

All Scripture quotations are taken from the *King James Version*.
Authorized King James Version.

Copyright © 2012 Melvin Phillips Jr.
All rights reserved.

ISBN 978-1-105-52769-2 (trade paper)

No part of this book may be used or reproduced in any manner whatsoever without written permission of the publisher, except in the case of brief quotations in articles and reviews. For information write: Kingdom Book & Gift LLP.,
P O Box 291975, Columbia, SC 29229.

Please visit our website for other great titles:
www.wix.com/trends/kingdombookandgift

For information regarding author interviews, please contact the publicity department via email
Kingdombookandgift@gmail.com

KB & G
Kingdom Book & Gift LLP
Publishers and Booksellers

The mission of this booklet is to glorify God by providing purposeful tools and products that will lift up and encourage the MAN and the Body of Christ. For those wrestling with Him.

*I dedicate this book to my inspiration,
my late but certainly great Mom,*
Dolores Phillips.

CONTENTS

I. THE KING AND I
(Wrestling with the Issues of a MAN)

A True Man's Challenges   07

Men who can't discuss emotions   13

II. THE KING AND THE ENEMY
(Wrestling with the Enemy of my soul)

Men, the Devil MUST obey YOU!   19

III. THE KING AND HIS WEAPONS
(Wrestling to use my weapons skill fully)

Praying Men!   25

IV. THE KING AND HIS CHILDREN
(Wresting to raise and train my seed)

A Father's Responsibility   32

Father's and their Children   37

V. THE KING AND HIS QUEEN
(Wrestling to become one)

The Husband Within Me   43

VI. THE KING AND SOCIETY
(Wresting with the cares of the world)

Men and Stress   49

VII. THE KING AND THE KINGDOM OF GOD
(Wrestling to be productive in the Kingdom)

Men, be a winner!   55

PART I.
THE KING AND I
(Wrestling with the Issues of a Man)

A TRUE MAN'S CHALLENGES EPH 5:16.

Greater love hath no man than this, that a man lay down his life for his friends. Ye are my friends, if ye do whatsoever I command you. Henceforth, I call you not servants; for the servant knoweth not what his Lord doeth; but I have called you friends; for all things that I have heard of my Father I have made known unto you. **(John 15: 13-15)**

The Old Testament prophet Amos once commanded God's people to hate that which is evil, and love God.

The Word of agreement flows easily from our mouths. Of course we hate evil and love what is good. We want to believe it. But (Amos) packed more into his command than we might grasp at first. Love- Hate. These verbs come packed with passion. Love embraces and holds tight.

Hate commits us to fight with our whole being. Do we hate evil and love good with that kind of zeal?

When I examine myself critically, I realize how seldom I truly hate what God hates and how seldom I am willing to take a stand for what God loves. A true man has challenges:

Job dealt with the challenge of grief after losing his children and all his possessions while he still praised God in his darkness. He also asked questions and sought answers. Finally, he submitted to God's wisdom and faithfulness and God doubled the blessings he had enjoyed early in life (Job 120:26). This was a true man. (Job 1:20-21)

Moses at age 80, assumed the leadership of God's people at God's direction. Moses felt ill-equipped to take on this challenge and he had some excuses for not wanting to accept God's call. The Lord had answers for all of Moses' objections. Matter of fact, he himself was the answer meeting Moses' needs.

Elijah also faced serious emotional and physical challenges. Depressed and exhausted, he saw no reason to continue on with his life. The Lord sent an angel to minister to him and he encouraged him that he was able to resume his ministry. This is yet another true man. (I Kings 19)

Paul struggled with an unnamed challenge that he called "his thorn in the flesh". For help he turned to the Lord. Even though the burden remained, he found comfort in the promise of Jesus. "My grace is sufficient for thee: for my strength is made perfect in weakness." (2 Corinthians 12:9)

And the greatest challenge of them all was when Jesus faced the challenge of serving his father here on earth by meeting the needs of the people around him. He found strength and guidance as he took time to get away by himself for prayer. Empowered by his father's love he endured the cross, conquering sin and death for us all. Now he brings us help and hope no matter how heavy the burdens we bear - no matter how trying our challenges may be. (Luke 5:15-16)

Kingdom Keys to Treasure

1. **Hate evil, but love God. Do both with passion.**
2. **Men must face challenges head on. They don't break you, they make you.**
3. **Let God's love be your fuel and reward.**

Study Notes

Study Notes

MEN WHO CAN'T DISCUSS EMOTIONS

Men don't talk about the emotions they feel. The problem with this inability to communicate forces the other spouse to become a mind reader. It puts additional burdens on the relationship. Tell the silent spouse the kind of emotional response you expect. It's not easy when you as the husband needs comforting. Usually this type of personality is not geared to comprehending another person's needs. Try to understand what makes your spouse act this way. Usually, it's the manner in which a person is raised that determines attitudes involving emotions.

Also, watch out for these mixed message syndromes. Your wish is my wish. This is a false accommodation intended to ingratiate or to avoid conflict. It makes the other person feel guilty or obligated to you. To love me is to know me. It's a false assumption that those nearest to us can drive our true wants and feelings. This syndrome is symptomatic of dependent people who dread rejection. I know what you're thinking. This is based on an utterly false notion that one can read an intimates mind. It enables the ostensible minded reader to projects his own thoughts and wants on the other then blame the spouse for not being satisfied.

Kingdom Keys to Treasure

1. You have emotions, don't let emotions have you.
2. Be transparent, stop trying to make people out to be mind readers.

Study Notes

Study Notes

PART II.
THE KING AND THE ENEMY
(Wrestling with the Enemy of my Soul)

MEN THE DEVIL MUST OBEY YOU!

MAT 7:29

When you stand on God's Word in the name of Jesus, the devil has to obey you. The main reason he will not obey you, is because you waiver in your faith. The devil will never obey a man or woman who waivers in their faith. The Bible says in James 1:6-8, "One who waivers will not receive from God."

If you ever find yourself fallen into any type of temptation repent immediately and ask the Lord for forgiveness. If you believe the Word and walk in faith without wavering, the Holy Spirit will empower you for victorious living.

Satan has no rights against you. He only rules and has legal rights to those who don't believe. John 14:12-14 says, "Verily, verily I say unto you, he that believeth on me, the words that I do shall he do also; and greater works than these shall he do; because I go unto My Father and whatsoever ye shall ask in my name that Will I do. That the Father may be glorified in the Son. If ye shall ask anything in my name I will do it."

> **Kingdom Keys to Treasure**
>
> 1. The devil is subject to the words that exit your lips.
> 2. The greater of God dwells in you, LET IT OUT!

Study Notes

Study Notes

PART III.
THE KING AND HIS WEAPONS
(Wrestling to use my weapons skilfully)

PRAYING MEN!

1 THESSA. 5:17.

"I exhort you therefore, that, first of all supplications, prayers, intercessions and giving of thanks be made for all men. For kings and for all that are in authority; that we may lead a quiet and peaceable life in all godliness and honesty for this is good and acceptable in the sight of God our Savior. I will (desire) therefore, that men pray everywhere, lifting up holy hands without wrath and doubt." (I Timothy 2:1-3, 8)

Men are to pray. All men are to pray. Men are distinguished from women. Men have strength in their wisdom. Jesus presented an absolute specific command that men should pray. It is absolutely imperative and necessary that men pray. Men were created first and because they are the first of human beings man should also be first in prayer.

Men are to pray for men. The direction in 1Timothy is specific and classifies we have specific direction with regard to women (I Timothy 2:9-12). In this scripture, the Bible deals with the men specifically and distinct from the women in relation to prayer, its importance, its idleness and its practice. Men are definitely commanded, seriously charged and strongly exhorted to pray.

Prayer succeeds when all else fails. Prayer has won great victories and has rescued God's saints with notable triumph when every other hope was gone. Men who know how to pray are the greatest. God gave men the greatest weapon and it is the power of prayer. Men who know how to use this weapon of prayer are God's best soldiers - His greatest leaders.

We are left with this only - praying hands can build the Kingdom of God. The men who pray are God's mighty ones on earth. They are His master builders. They may be destitute of all else but with the wrestling and prevailing of a simple heart of faith and prayer, they are mightily the mightiest for God.

Men of prayer are needed especially in the positions of Church influence, honor and power. Leaders of Churches should always manifest a demonstration of the manifestation of prayer. James 5:17-18. James was a man subject to like passions as we are and he prayed earnestly that it might not rain and it rained not on the earth by the space of thee years and six months. And he prayed again and the heaven gave rain and the earth brought forth her fruit.

Kingdom Keys to Treasure

1. Men ought to pray and pray often.

2. When all else fails — strength, words, intellect, creativity — pray.

Study Notes

Study Notes

PART IV.
THE KING AND HIS CHILDREN
(Wrestling to raise and train my seed)

A FATHER'S RESPONSIBILITY

COL. 3:21.

Children look to their fathers for support and guidance. A father needs to have the right concept of life and of the influences and associations that should surround his family. Above all, he should be controlled by the love and fear of God and by the teachings of His Word that he may guide the feet of his children in the right way.

The father is the lawmaker of the household and like Abraham he should make the law of God the rule of his home. God said to Abraham I know him, that he will command his children and his household. (Genesis 18:19)

Fathers, let your children see that you love them and will do all you can in your power to make them happy. If you do this your necessary restrictions will have far greater weight in their young minds. Rule your children with tenderness and compassion, remembering they are angels. Do always behold the face of my father which is in heaven. (Matthew 18:10)

If you desire them to do the work given to them by God, cooperate with them by doing your part.

Kingdom Keys to Treasure

1. Fathers are a child's first vision of God..
2. Don't provoke your children to wrath, love them to life.

Study Notes

Study Notes

FATHER'S AND THEIR CHILDREN

(6)CHP- TIT 2:7

Why are kids always hating parents one minute and desperately seeking heart to heart talks the next? Trying on new personality types and behavioral patterns then discarding them, worrying about society and the cosmos one minute and becoming overcome with personal agonies the next.

It's not helpful to ask: What's the matter with you? Or why can't you sit still? What has suddenly gotten into you? They don't want instant understanding. Don't pretend to know how they feel. They can't believe that we as parents were teenagers or felt the same way at one time in our lives. Confronted with these annoying traits it's best to develop tolerance, but also make it clear that acceptance does not always mean approval.

Never emulate teenagers' language or conduct. They deliberately adopt a lifestyle that is different from their parents. Such emulation drives children into opposition. Every child has some imperfections about which he or she is overly sensitive. Be very careful not to reinforce them. Young children will soon enough torment their peers with name calling, however, insults cut deeper and last longer when they came from a father or mother. Even in jesting, it's wiser not to tease them.

Don't preach or lecture to your children. Never use reverse psychology or predictions on them either saying things like 'You'll never be able to hold a job unless you learn to get up on time." Avoid confusion or contradictory messages. It's better to share a clear prohibition.

Study Notes

Study Notes

PART V.
THE KING AND HIS QUEEN
(Wrestling to become ONE)

THE HUSBAND WITHIN ME!

CHP-CO 7:3.

Jesus gives life to a new community of love – the Church. The Church is His own body. His love of the Church also defines the marriage relationship between a man and a woman for His people. Paul teaches that the genders are complementary and a man and a woman are equal before God. Yet in marriage the husband has the leadership role. This leadership is not absolute but gives the husband the initiative in marriage to which the wife responds. "Wives submit to your own husbands as to the Lord for the husband is the head of the wife as also Christ is the head of the church and He is the Savior of the body. Therefore just as the church is subject to Christ so let the wives be to their own husbands in everything. Husbands love your wives just as Christ also loves the Church and gave himself for her that he might sanctify and cleanse her with the washing of water by the word that he might present her to himself a glorious church not having spot or wrinkle or any such thing but that she should be holy and without blemish." (Ephesians 5:22-28)

Paul outlines in these verses the entire process to which Christ has forged a relationship with the Church. He has washed her from sin and is intimate and joined the church to himself through the bonds of the covenant he fulfilled and this intimate union forms an analogy for Christian marriages.

Kingdom Keys to Treasure

1. Love your wife, as Christ loves the Church. With an everlasting love.

Study Notes

Study Notes

PART VI.
THE KING AND SOCIETY
(Wrestling with the Cares of the World)

MEN AND STRESS!

It's easy to recognize when you have already pushed yourself too far - you are sick, exhausted, or just miserable – it's more difficult recognizing that you are beginning to overdo. Catching yourself before stress catches you. There are early wavering signs that life is becoming too stressful for your own capacities to adapt to pressure. But we often ignore the signals. Work ethic tells us to work hard and not pamper ourselves. Instead of heeding the inner voice when it says too much. We answer back. I can handle anything.

Strong emotions without apparent cause everyone is unhappy for some reason at times. However, when you feel depressed, angry or irritable and nothing in particular has occurred you emotionsare telling you that you are under more stress than you know how to handle comfortably.

Stand fast therefore in the liberty where with Christ has made you free and do not be entangled again with the yoke of bondage. (Galatians 5:1)

Kingdom Keys to Treasure

1. Catch yourself before stress catches you.
2. Know when too much is too much.

Study Notes

Study Notes

PART VII.
THE KING AND KINGDOM OF GOD
(Wrestling to be Productive in the Kingdom)

MEN, BE A WINNER!

Some people have an unmistakable aura of success because they have really made it. But those on the way up can look like winners if a few basic tactics are followed.

Stay current. Read the right papers and magazines. And never attend a social gathering without being prepared with something to contribute to the conversation.

Men meet important people. Look for chances to make right contacts and join the right groups, professional associations, charities and churches. Go all out to meet the right people. Don't be bashful.

Try to answer correspondence within 24 hours of receipt. It gives the impression of being on top of the job. Act like you belong. Whether you are in a boardroom or at the White House. Don't whisper or look down. Look people in the eye. When you do you automatically take the lead in a conversation when you don't you're letting someone else take the lead.

Kingdom Keys to Treasure

1. You were born to win, and ordained to lead. So GO DO IT.
2. Today is a good day to begin again. Go with God this time.

Study Notes

Study Notes